FREEDOM, VULNERABILITY, and LOVE:

A Journey of Self Discovery

KATHY BAZINET

BALBOA PRESS
A DIVISION OF HAY HOUSE

Copyright © 2014 Kathy Bazinet.

All rights reserved. No part of this book may be used or reproduced by any means, graphic, electronic, or mechanical, including photocopying, recording, taping or by any information storage retrieval system without the written permission of the publisher except in the case of brief quotations embodied in critical articles and reviews.

Balboa Press books may be ordered through booksellers or by contacting:

Balboa Press
A Division of Hay House
1663 Liberty Drive
Bloomington, IN 47403
www.balboapress.com
1 (877) 407-4847

Because of the dynamic nature of the Internet, any web addresses or links contained in this book may have changed since publication and may no longer be valid. The views expressed in this work are solely those of the author and do not necessarily reflect the views of the publisher, and the publisher hereby disclaims any responsibility for them.

The author of this book does not dispense medical advice or prescribe the use of any technique as a form of treatment for physical, emotional, or medical problems without the advice of a physician, either directly or indirectly. The intent of the author is only to offer information of a general nature to help you in your quest for emotional and spiritual well-being. In the event you use any of the information in this book for yourself, which is your constitutional right, the author and the publisher assume no responsibility for your actions.

Any people depicted in stock imagery provided by Thinkstock are models,
and such images are being used for illustrative purposes only.
Certain stock imagery © Thinkstock.

Printed in the United States of America.

ISBN: 978-1-4525-1773-5 (sc)
ISBN: 978-1-4525-1775-9 (hc)
ISBN: 9781-4525-1774-2 (e)

Library of Congress Control Number: 2014911847

Balboa Press rev. date: 07/08/2014

To Hailey and Samantha. None of this would have been possible without your love, support, and encouragement. Thank you for always believing in me. You make my world a better place!

Preface

This past August, I woke one day to the realization there was a plan in place for my life that made no sense to me. The plan included where I would live, work, spend my vacations, and how I would parent. The shocking truth was this plan was not aligned with who I really was or who I wanted to be. How had this happened? I had actively participated in each decision leading up to that point, but I felt like I was a stranger in my own life. When this realization hit me, I made some quick and dramatic changes in my life, all within a short period of time.

As painful as these changes were, I knew deep within they were needed, and in the end, all of us would be better off. My eldest daughter's wise words were playing out in my life:

> If the rate of external change exceeds your rate of internal growth, change will be forced upon you. And typically not in a way that is preferred or comfortable.

Freedom, Vulnerability, and Love: A Journey of Self-Discovery is a collection of my writing that captures my transformation over six months as I dealt with the fallout of my decisions and truly learned to love my life. Below is a synopsis of what I learned. Knowing these truths are one thing, but living them will be daily practice:

- The world is a beautiful place and each of us has the ability to make it even more beautiful. When we do it together, the synergy is where the magic happens.

- Letting go is not easy, but it is probably one of the greatest gifts you can give yourself.
- Sometimes the darkest moments are where you discover your greatest truths.
- Trust starts with yourself. When you trust yourself, you discover that all the answers are already within you.
- Freedom is a state of mind, and the environment is just the backdrop. Choose to experience freedom in all that you do.
- Vulnerability does not make you weak. It can be your greatest strength.
- Love is easy! When it is not easy, then it is attachment.
- Forgiveness is more about what *you* need than it is about the other person. Be generous with forgiveness, and your heart and soul will thank you.
- Failure is an option, and it is worth the risk.
- Remember to always love yourself. You are worth it. Keep your life choices aligned with this knowing. Remember that the little choices add up. Don't ever settle!
- Everyone has his or her own truth. Live yours. Know that others will follow their own truth. Trust that those who are aligned with your truth will remain in your life and those who are not will leave. Do not take things so personally.
- Discomfort means you are growing. In the discomfort, it is easy to forget, but do what it takes to remember that love is the answer for everything.

I have included a section after each journal entry called "Behind the Writing" in an effort to share what—and how—I was learning at the time. It is my hope that this will be useful to you in your own journey of self-discovery into freedom, vulnerability, and love.

With love,
Kathy

Acknowledgments

Thank you to my two beautiful, spirited, and inspiring daughters, Hailey and Samantha. Each of you in your own way has taught me so much in this life. I am so grateful for the countless hours Hailey spent helping with edits and for how Samantha waited with loving patience on many nights for me to wrap up my writing so she could have her time with me. I cherish their unwavering dedication and support. I love you both to the moon and back.

Thank you, Matt, for providing me with the setting in which so much of this learning has come to the surface and for the use of the wonderful photos.

Loving thanks to both my parents, Mick and Irene, and my brother Ray for encouragement and practical support while I took on this latest adventure. You mean the world to the girls and me.

I am grateful to Laurie, my wonderful and amazing peer coach. When I first approached her in late August with the idea of peer coaching, I was not sure where it would take us. Not only did she trust the idea, she jumped in with enthusiasm and support. Each week, Laurie has helped keep me on track with my goals, has provided valuable reflection on my experiences, and has quickly become a dear and trusted friend.

I am filled with deep gratitude for René for reminding me to trust myself and for providing the environment to explore my newfound freedom, vulnerability, and love.

To Caroline, Brad, Vitu, Amarpreet, Kristen, Lindsay O, Hermian, and Lindsay SD, thank you for your constant and sometimes daily encouragement and cheer.

Each of you believed in me and believed in my writing *Freedom, Vulnerability, And Love: A Journey of Self-Discovery* long before I did. From the bottom of my heart, I am forever grateful.

(Photo credit: Matt Symes)

Contents

Freedom 1
    Freedom, Sweet Freedom 3
    Finding Comfort without Control 7
    Immediate Action versus Patience 13
    Patience—Faking It until You Make It 17
    Failure Is an Option 21
    Finding My Way 25
    In Gratitude 27
    Riding the Wave of Adventure 31
    Reframing My Story 35

Vulnerability 39
    Vulnerability 41
    Embracing the Language of the Heart 45
    Emotions—Embracing the Human Experience 49
    Hide-and-Seek with Happiness 51
    Anger from Deep Within 55
    From the Darkness, There Is Peace 59
    Vulnerability Wants to Play 63

Love 67
    Just Breathe 69
    The Gift of Love 73
    The Power of Believing and Loving Your Life 77

I Love You!...79
Always Meant to Be 83
For a Moment, I Was Lost in Wonderland 87
Standing Close to the Edge 91

The Journey Continues 95
Living Life Fully..97

Freedom

*Our thoughts can be the cage that traps
us or the key that frees us!*

Freedom, Sweet Freedom

In August 2013, I woke one day to realize my lifelong journey of self-discovery was about to take another significant turn. I had lost my way again; I had lost my freedom.

Freedom. Sweet freedom. We met, embraced, danced, and vowed never to part. Slowly, very slowly, we grew apart, despite my promise to never leave you. The times we visited became fewer and fewer, until one day, I woke up and realized I had lost my way again. I had lost you, sweet freedom.

I know it is a bit dramatic, but I recently realized that freedom is a state of mind and the environment is only the backdrop. It sounds so simple, but the concept was lost on me my entire life! I think that might be where I got confused so many years ago.

I only experienced glimpses of freedom in extreme sports and adventures, but not in my daily life. For the most part, I had always done what was expected of me. I have worked long, hard hours to pay for a house, a car, and family vacations. I have strived to be Supermom by almost singlehandedly organizing a large school fun fair, volunteering for countless kid-related organizations, running from one sports activity to another, and essentially taking on so much that sleeping became less and less of an option. I did that because it was what a loving, dedicated mother is supposed to do, right?

I was promoted at work and moved into a high-pressure role, despite the fact that I did not want the promotion. I tried to be the best daughter/sister/friend that I could be, and so on and so on. I lived my life based on what other people expected of me, what society said I should do, and what I thought was right.

I did have a brief moment in my life when I came face-to-face with the state of freedom. When I remembered what my soul knew to be true. I knew in that moment that I could live in a state of freedom, regardless of the scenery.

In 2008, I was diagnosed with multiple sclerosis. At thirty-eight, I was the executive director of a nonprofit organization and a single mother of two beautiful, active, and spirited girls. I was constantly on the go. I could easily have been crowned "Independent Woman of the Year." The diagnosis was a blow beyond anything I had ever experienced.

I immediately decided to take some time off from work to create a care plan for myself. How would I begin making a care plan for a single mom who would soon become highly dependent on others? I had always enjoyed adventures and pushing myself beyond my comfort zone, but I knew I needed a spiritual awakening. I needed something that would shake up my world, help me see my life differently, and something to move me from seeing my future as doomed.

I called a friend and said, "Have you ever considered skydiving?"

A few days later, I found myself in the door of an airplane, fourteen thousand feet above the earth, ready to take a leap of faith. *I trust! I trust in this moment I am dependent on another with my life. I free myself of needing to be so independent that I forget all the wonderful gifts needing gives. I release myself to really live!*

As we left the plane, I was in complete awe. I forgot that I was supposed to smile for the camera guy. I forgot that I was falling at 120 miles per hour. I forgot that I was afraid of what tomorrow would bring. Instead, I couldn't take my eyes off the ground, in awe, in appreciation, in a state of pure joy. I trusted my instructor to take care of me. I trusted myself to do my required tasks, and I trusted the experience. It was the ultimate sense of freedom!

Eighteen months later, so much of my life had been transformed and, from that, one of the gifts was my neurologist clearing me; my brain was cured.

I knew freedom! How over the next three short years did I forget it? How did I get to where I am today? I slowly went back to my work routine, and life's perceived expectations started to fall back into place.

Today, without having to jump from a plane, I am embracing (or more accurately, *remembering*) the realization that freedom is a state of mind—and the physical environment is just the setting. Today, at the end of one of my meetings, I went for a walk to the store. I left my desk and did not feel guilty that I lost twenty minutes of work.

As I walked to my car at the end of the day, I smiled to each person I passed on the street with no expectation that any of them would smile back at me. I did it because it felt good. When I got home, I played loud music and danced wildly in my kitchen, despite the fact that my neighbor was cutting his lawn and likely could hear and see me. There it was again—freedom, my sweet freedom!

Behind the Writing

The idea that freedom is a state of mind and the environment is just the backdrop seems so simple. And when you change the way you think, it truly becomes that easy. Having said that, this is a daily practice for me, and some days are easier than others.

As I wrote the above journal entry, I was just days into starting my first blog. There was something freeing about being honest, real, and just me—in a very public way! The experience quickly became healing. It was not only the act of journaling; the sharing with others was awakening my connection to my soul.

Whether creating a blog or using a personal journal, I have found that daily writing provides a rich resource to look back on and understand patterns of thoughts and behaviors. It provides an opportunity to look for consistencies and contradictions in thoughts and behaviors and an opportunity to view the gap between where one currently is versus where one would like to be (to explore who I *am* versus who I wish to be).

Take a minimum of ten minutes out of your day to capture your thoughts. Some questions to get you started might be:

- What did you learn about yourself today?
- What does freedom mean to you?
- Does the thought of sharing your experience with others in a public forum, such as a blog, appeal to you? Why or why not? If not, is it because of fear?
- How is fear a barrier to your sense of freedom?
- How does fear block your experience of freedom in your day-to-day experiences?
- How well do you really know yourself?

Consider how you might want to capture these thoughts: in a journal, a blog, or in an e-mail to a close friend. Take action today. Do just one thing that stirs that sense of freedom within you. Consider all that you might learn about yourself as you journey along with me.

Finding Comfort without Control

I have a confession to make, which I am sure will shock many people in my life. My greatest fear is loss of control! Yep. There it is. I said it. I am a control freak! I have done an incredible job of convincing myself over the last few years that I love the *mystery* of the unknown. However, now that I am staring into the unknown, I realize I do not feel excitement, anticipation, or joy. Instead, I feel sad, uneasy, and even irritated.

Do not get me wrong. I have many tools in my toolbox to help me talk myself back into feeling good, but in doing so, I take myself out of the mysterious unknown. When I sit in the unknown, all my bad habits about exercising control come flooding back. This time, I am ready to fight back. I know the difference this time, and I know I must learn to do it differently. Since I value honesty so much, I should also fess up and say that I am probably the only one who really is shocked by how much I fear loss of control. After working on an exercise about personal values and personal pain values, I realized how much power the fear of loss of control actually has over my life.

Over the years, I have had tiny moments of insight and understanding about this, but I am only starting to realize its full impact. One glimpse into this happened a few years back when I started rock climbing. At first, I thought I was afraid of falling, but then realized I could jump from a plane from fourteen thousand feet above the earth and fall at 120 miles per hour, but I could not fall a few feet from the ground when I was climbing. What was the difference? When I skydive, I get to decide the exact moment in which I jump out of the plane. When I fall off the rock face, I have no control over it. It just happens!

As I continue to write on my journey of self-discovery, I am becoming more aware of how strong a motivator the fear of loss of control is in my life. I am realizing it has had way too much influence on significant decisions and has likely robbed me of many rich experiences. When faced with a loss of control, I go into "manage it" mode. At times, I manage it at any cost.

I am beginning to understand how many opportunities I have missed through the years: meeting new people, getting to really know the people in my life, job choices/opportunities, adventures, and possibly my passion. If I could not be instantly great at something—or control the outcome of it—I chose the more comfortable path, the one I knew (or thought) I could control.

I have only ever taken on that which I already knew I could handle. In my adventures and extreme sports, it appeared that I relished the loss of control. However, the truth is that I studied, practiced, and knew my stuff so well that the risk of losing control was so minimized that I could fool myself into believing it did not exist. In all other aspects of my life, if I did not feel in control, I figured out how to push away, change my mind, or even convince myself that it was not what I wanted anyway. Pretending fear and control had nothing to do with it.

Recently, I attended a five-day conference that started with a yoga class every day. The yoga class was not like any I had ever taken before; we did yoga through dance. The second-to-last dance each day was on the celebration of chaos. It celebrated the loss of control. On the first day, I danced around and watched the others let loose. I actually found it to be quite entertaining. I just mimicked them and pretended to let go.

On the second day, I figured I could not possibly look as silly as most of the other folks in the room. I closed my eyes and attempted to lose control. I was shocked by how hard it was for me. I was in a conference room, with others of like mind, safe, but I could not relax into the dance of chaos.

By day three, I decided if I could travel that far and spend that much money, then I sure as heck could take on the opportunity to experience loss of control in a pretty safe environment. I danced the dance of chaos. My body flailed in all directions, stomped, screamed, jerked around, and bumped into people. Oh my, did it feel good.

To my surprise, I broke down into sobs; not just the odd tear, it was full-on ugly/beauty cry. Tears flowed as though the dam broke; booger juice and snot were streaming out from my nose, running along the upper edge of my lip. The flood of tears dampened the ends of my hair, snorting sounds escaped my lips, and my body heaved as I gave up all control. For a moment, I tasted the sweetness of freedom and vulnerability. When I left the conference, I forgot again!

Comfort with the unknown, the mystery, and loss of control. Just typing and saying these words aloud put my stomach into knots. My neck and shoulders tightened up and adrenaline raged through my veins. I was sitting safely in my own home and typing on my computer, but my ego told me I was capable of staying in control. My body begged me to understand that I needed to let go.

From the personal/pain values exercise and my experience with the dance of chaos, I was beginning to understand that the action of holding on so tightly had likely caused me a lot of heartbreak, loss, and sadness in my life. In order to fully embrace freedom, vulnerability, and love, I needed to learn to accept and embrace the realization that many of the details of my life were out of my control. My job was to set the compass, feel and embrace the passion, and let the pieces fall into place.

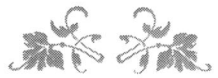

Behind the Writing

Personal values are the core beliefs, values, and philosophies that we hold for our lives and our life purposes. As we grow up, we take on others' values; when we reach our teen years, we start to accept or reject the values that define who we are. For many of us, it is easy to accept the values that are put on us by parents, teachers, culture, or society. Taking the time to know, question, and determine what we value is important because it shapes our decisions—even the really small ones that determine how we live each of our days. Our pain values are the values we have accepted that are unsupportive or even disruptive in our lives.

When I took the time to explore my personal values and pain values, I was surprised to realize how much of my life was directed by my fears. Take some time to explore your life values and your pain values. The more you know yourself on a deep level, the more empowered you become in creating and guiding your life.

Life Values and Pain Values Exercise

Take some time to explore examples of life values and pain values (you can find many examples on the Internet). See which ones feel right for you. What personal values seem aligned with your life? Make a note of each value that feels right to you and take some time to understand the definition of each one. Try to reduce your list to ten if you can. Now do the same for the pain values, but try to keep your list to five. Fifteen seems to be a manageable number of values to use as your guide.

Once you have your fifteen, create a personal rule statement for each one. Then write down what daily behaviors you will practice in order to move your life forward in the direction you desire. Below are some examples of my life value/pain value statements and rules:

My personal definition of *freedom* is to embrace freedom in all that I do, to remember that freedom is a state of mind, and to find joy in all that I do, even when I am not enjoying the ride. I keep my thoughts in the present moment.

My personal rules for *freedom* are to experience freedom by making decisions that are best for me first (from a heart-opened place), to work toward removing myself from any situation I cannot find myself living in a state of freedom, and to recognize when I am out of alignment with my values.

My daily practice is to continue journaling/blogging/writing each day, especially when I am in a funk, to do an active meditation each day, such as staying fully present while walking, doing dishes, or exercising.

My personal definition of *zest for life* is adventure and playfulness in all that I do, and having the desire to give my all toward living my dreams.

My personal rules for *zest for life* are to find opportunities to be playful each day, to clarify or redefine my dreams and set goals to achieve these dreams four times a year, and seek out adventures every month.

My daily practice is to explore or engage in something solely for the purpose of play at least once a day.

My personal pain value of *loss of control*—feeling I have no say, or as if life is happening to me.

My personal rules for *loss of control* are to meditate daily, to practice yoga when I am stressed, and to avoid talking too much in stressful situations since this gives me a false sense of control.

My daily practice is to stop and examine what I am trying to control when I feel my body tense, my stomach toss, or my teeth clench. I will repeat my mantra and say, "I surrender."

My personal pain value of *betrayal* is being cheated, rejected, or humiliated.

My personal rule for betrayal is to remind myself that I am enough—and I can walk away from this behavior in my life.

My daily practice includes journaling about and exploring why I am enough. I also look at myself in the mirror each morning and say, "I love you."

The first step to change is awareness. The second step is putting daily habits in place to create positive changes—one step at a time. What have you discovered about your life values? Your pain values? Are you being guided by the values and daily habits you desire? Is your life happening *to* you or *by* you?

Immediate Action versus Patience

Today, I am realizing I need a lesson with patience, but just typing the word made me feel rather impatient. Long ago, I decided patience did not serve me well, and despite the number of times I was reminded to have patience, I still had no real relationship with it.

I think the majority of people in my life (please keep in mind that I, for the most part, had done a great job of keeping people at a safe distance) would say I am a very patient person. But while I am pretending to be patient, my inner voice is screaming, "Just get on with it! I want to know the answer now! I want to know the next steps now! I want the plan now! I need to know what is going to happen now." Yep, no patience. It was probably closely tied to my need to (falsely) believe I had any real "control."

Somewhere along the line, I mistakenly thought patience meant not taking action. If I did not take immediate action, I thought I would miss out on opportunities or things would go from good to gone. My belief became twisted, and I thought learning to embrace moments of patience would somehow remove my ability to take immediate action. Over the years, I have come to know the good side of immediate action. As a result, I chose to embrace and practice immediate action and hold those success stories up as proof that it was the better choice or even the only choice.

I have locked some of my immediate action success stories into my being. When I was five, I was hiking with my family up a mountain. We were high up on one of the trails when my two-year-old brother got to close to the edge of the path and slipped over. Within a split second, I managed to grab his hand and held him as he dangled over the side. I held on for dear life until my parents, just seconds later, grabbed us both. This many years later, I still have a clear memory of how my hand grasped his hand. I can still feel the sweat in my palms as my body instantly reacted in fear. The tree bark cut into my other hand as I grasped the handrail above me. The dust and dirt scratched at my eyes, but I knew if I let go—or I couldn't hold on—I would be responsible for my brother's likely death. At that moment, the understanding that immediate action was the only way to get what you needed or wanted was burned into my very being. We still laugh at how I saved Ray's life in that moment. Behind the laughs, there is a deep appreciation for my quick action. We know how easily all our lives could have been different had I not responded with such quickness.

There was another time when immediate action and I became intimate with one another. When I was a teenager, my mom was cooking dinner on a gas stove. Her sweater caught on fire, and my mom froze. Despite the fact that the flame was quickly moving up the back of her sweater, she did not move a muscle. As it neared her long dark hair, my dad froze in his seat at the table. His jaw dropped, and his eyes were wide with fear.

I felt like time was moving in slow motion. Simultaneously, I could bear witness to their shock, noticed my brother's lack of awareness, and watched the blue flame climb the black fuzzy sweater. I was able to process all of this information, and within a few seconds, I jumped to my feet and pulled the sweater off of my mom in one quick motion. I stomped on it until the flames went out.

There are countless other times in my life—and many a lot less dramatic—that speak to the incredible value of taking immediate action. For tonight, I will say, "Immediate action, thank you for all the gifts/opportunities/valued results you have given me. Thank you for the successes I have achieved and could never have achieved had you not been there for me. Although at this time I am venturing out to meet your counterpart, patience, you and I will remain very near and dear friends.

Behind the Writing

Take some time to explore the role of patience and the role of action in your life. Writing out your thoughts can help provide clarity and understanding. Explore the following questions in your journal or blog:

- Are you a person of action or a person of patience?
- Have you discovered the balance between the two?
- What value does action play in your life?
- What value does patience play in your life?
- What are you learning about yourself by journaling?
- Are you doing things differently in your life?

If freedom is a state of mind and the environment the backdrop, take some time to explore whether you are the type of person where action helps or hinders your sense of personal freedom?

In addition to exploring the above questions, you might want to consider the valuable exercise of creating your own vision board. A vision board is made of pictures or words depicting what you want for your future to serve as a daily visual reminder and motivator. The vision board is an exercise in the design of your future and the action of implementing daily habits that will move you to your desired state. It also requires the art and acceptance of patience as you move from where you are to where you want to be. I have taped my vision board to the back of my bedroom door; it is the last thing I see before sleep and the first upon waking in the morning.

My vision board includes many statements. *I experience financial freedom. I experience freedom in my daily living. I experience time freedom.*

I experience ease and flow in all that I do (the practice of patience). My vision board has pictures of tangible things I want to manifest in my life. With each statement, I have a daily habit in order to achieve the desired state.

In addition to a paper copy, I have also created a four-minute vision video. I used photos that articulate my dreams/goals/aspiration, reminders of the required daily habits, and inspiring words in a slideshow with a motivating song. I view the video at least once a week as a motivating reminder of my dreams!

Take some time to create your own vision board or vision video. There are many wonderful examples on the Internet. Knowing what you want is the first step. Once you have that in place, you can start to create the daily habits that will take you there. If you would like to explore these ideas in greater detail or if you are struggling to implement any of these strategies, book a complementary session with me to determine how I may further support and serve you – www.kathybazinet.com (coaching)

Patience—Faking It until You Make It

I am coming to understand the value of patience in my life. And despite my discomfort with the experience of waiting, it is time I learn this valuable skill. Although there have been many times in my life when immediate action has served me well, there have also been many times when it has backfired and had a negative impact on my life.

Many missed adventures, missed relationships, missed friendships, missed experiences, and missed career opportunities because I never took the time or had the patience to really explore what I wanted in life. I didn't dig deep to know myself and didn't allow the time and space for the best possible answers to rise from within to the surface.

Instead, my compulsive need to act and my disrespectful disregard for the value of patience (and the time that comes with slowing down) has determined the direction of my life to a large degree. Don't get me wrong; I have been blessed in my life and consider myself to be relatively successful (from the lens of societal standards), but I hunger for more. I have tasted a different way of living, and I yearn for it. I am willing to do the work it takes to experience life in its fullest. That includes practicing patience and a trust that, with patience, some of the juiciest answers/opportunities/desires will come to the surface. When that happens, it will be time for action.

Patience, I know we will become good friends in time, despite my discomfort. But for today, the stillness of patience is almost painful. I am aware of my physical reaction to the discomfort; instead of trying to move into action, I will sit in patience. I will meditate despite my mind/ego screaming at me. I will focus on saying, "Let go. I surrender, release, and move into ease and flow." I will trust sometimes that the universe/situations/people need space and time to sort out the details.

My nemesis, patience, I welcome you into my life. I am aware that I am faking it until I make it, but for today, I would like to get to know you better so I can enjoy the beautiful dance of balance between patience and action. I know my life will be so much richer in the end for this knowing.

> "Patience is not the ability to wait but the ability to keep a good attitude while waiting." —Joyce Meyer

Behind the Writing

The subconscious mind is incredibly powerful. It stores every interaction and experience we have ever had. The subconscious mind guides our current behaviors based on past experiences. Repeating new messages can change the subconscious mind.

I have also come to see the value of routine and creating healthy daily habits. These routines help in the intentional reprogramming of the subconscious mind. One example of this would be the daily practice of a five-minute morning and evening routine. These five-minute routines require action, but it is the daily practice and patience that see the results. Some examples of these five-minute practices are:

- When your alarm goes off in the morning, do a counting mediation. Resist the temptation to allow your mind to race ahead to the upcoming day's activities. Simply count backward from fifty. Visualize each number individually. Focus your thoughts.

- Listen to an audio clip of affirmations, inspirational stories, or inspirational songs, while showering. I highly recommend searching on YouTube for Abraham Hicks. The clips vary between five and twenty minutes in length.
- Review your vision board or vision video.
- Do a gratitude prayer.
- Learn something new each day. Read a self-help book each day, watch a TEDx video (found on the Internet), listen to a motivational CD, or watch a documentary.

Creating daily habits will start to move you in the direction of your dreams. Changing our habits and subconscious thoughts takes patience. Knowing, appreciating, and making peace with the slow but valuable process is patience at its best.

Failure Is an Option

My ego is well aware that failure/mistakes are supposed to be a good thing. It is a sign of action, trying, and effort, and no true success can ever be accomplished without some level of failure. Thomas Edison failed close to ten thousand times before he invented the lightbulb. In his mind, he created ten thousand ways that the lightbulb did not work. Why, despite all my years of self-exploration, do I still fear failure? Somehow, time and time again, I have survived failure. Many of my best learning experiences have been in the moments when failure looked me right in the eyes and kicked me in the behind.

Here is one of my many stories of failure. I have mentioned that I have enjoyed skydiving. What I have not mentioned yet is that my nickname from the sport is Wally—a nickname given to me after my first experience of failure with jumping. Skydiving has given me many amazing opportunities, glimpses of freedom, the feeling of being fully alive, the value of facing my fears, and an appreciation of all that is learned in the experience of failure. Failing in skydiving is not something typically you would want to call to your life. When I explained to the triage nurse that my injuries were due to a skydiving accident, I was well aware of how serious failure in this sport really is. (An operating room was booked, and I was then fast-tracked through the emergency department, despite my constant protest that I was certain at most I had a small crack in my ankle.)

On my second solo dive (my fifth overall), I wore a one-way radio. I could hear my coach, but he could not hear me. As I was coming in to prepare for landing, his instructions seemed odd. They seemed to be in direct contrast to the instructions I had received during our dirt dive (practice dive on the ground). I did what I often do. I ignored all the red flags that my intuition, gut, and body were sending and listened to another. I did not know my angle skewed my coach's depth perception. He did not realize I was as low as I was—or that I was as far back as I was. I knew not to cross the road and get myself over the hydro lines, but I did.

As a result, I flew in low over the parking lot and headed straight toward a building. Despite the larger grass landing area just a few feet away, I managed to hit the building. I had been trained well and knew exactly how to hit something. I flared at the exact moment I needed to. In order to avoid the railing, I lifted my legs at the exact moment I needed too, and then I gently hit the building. It felt surreal as I slowly slid down the side of the building (almost like a cartoon character) and sat on my bottom.

I failed big time on that jump! I failed to listen to my own experience, failed to find a safe place to land, and failed to follow the rule of not crossing over the hydro lines. In that failing, I learned so much. Following Thomas Edison's line of thinking, I learned how to hit a building and survive! I got back at it the next season after spending a couple of months on crutches. When I jumped again, the experience was even sweeter. I learned that my desires are stronger than my fear of failure!

It was a beautiful lesson, and I still hold it close to my heart on my journey of self-discovery. My ego still screams, "You are going to fail. Who are you to think you can do that? Can you really live with that failure?"

I answer, "Yes! I sure can!" Not trying is the real failure! Failure is an option, and it is worth the risk.

Behind the Writing

When my girls were much younger and would make a mistake, they would often yell "Failure." It apparently was a cool way of laughing off the mistake. With much convincing, our family decided to change the statement from failure to *learning opportunity.*

I have come to realize that I learn just as much—if not more—from my mistakes as I ever have from my successes. The stories we tell ourselves determine whether we have supportive thoughts or unsupportive thoughts. Remember that freedom is a state of mind—and the environment is just the backdrop. Failure really is another learning opportunity. Take time to explore some of the failures/learning opportunities you have had in your life.

- What have your learned from your latest failure/learning opportunity?
- Would you do it differently next time? Why or why not?
- What value did this experience add to your life?
- When you change your language from failure to learning opportunity, does that change your perspective of the experience?

Finding My Way

When I look back to just a few months ago, I question how I was so lost. I had actively participated in every decision in my life that had led to that point, yet I still woke one day and wondered how I got there. Hindsight is twenty-twenty, and I now realize

- I stopped listening to my own needs and wants and surrendered my life to another without even realizing it;
- when I partnered I gave it my all—my house, my money, my vacations, my time, my goals, my dreams—until one day I woke up exhausted, depleted, and lost;
- I ignored the truths that presented themselves over and over again right in front of me until I no longer trusted myself;
- I waited for unanswered promises to manifest into physical form until I could no longer remember what it was I was waiting for; and
- I allowed another to convince me I was an improvement project until I felt I would never be good enough and was a failure.

In every experience, there are many blessings. Over the last few months, I have learned that

- being lost is an opportunity to find my way and the chance to redefine my life;
- it is important to remember my dreams and to have the courage to dream even bigger;

- I am capable of seeing beauty in all that I experience, even in the uncomfortable moments;
- I am perfect in all of my imperfections, and knowing this is freeing;
- I can forgive others;
- I can forgive myself; and
- I have the capacity to love my world.

Freedom is the gift that comes from knowing yourself and following your own path despite the obstacles. Freedom, we are becoming wonderful friends.

Behind the Writing

British journalist Alexander Hamilton said, "If you don't stand for something, then you will fall for anything." This is a good reminder of the importance of truly knowing who and what you want in your life—regardless of your current circumstances.

Do you know what you stand for? Explore when and where you stray from staying true to your personal values? When do your pain values seem to control your behaviors and actions?

Refer back to the earlier exercise where you created the rules for how you will manage your pain values when they surface? Have you created and implemented the daily practices? How can you improve on these? What is one thing you will do today to start implementing those practices?

In Gratitude

Never let the things you want make
you forget the things you have.
—Author unknown

In the wee hours of this morning, like so many others, I woke long before my alarm. As I enjoyed the warmth of my bed and the cuddles from my puppy, I listed off what I was grateful for on this wonderful journey I call my life. In my pursuit of me, in my conquest for self-discovery, and while digging for a glimpse of my inner truth to remember, I learned to be thankful for all that I have already!

I am thankful that my youngest daughter did her chores yesterday with only one reminder. Last night, my eldest daughter jumped with excitement as she headed to her competitive rock-climbing class, and she stayed an extra two hours with the same enthusiasm.

This morning, as I watched the rain come down outside my window, I was thankful to have a warm bed, a roof over my head, hot water that is easily accessible, a closet full of a variety of clothes to choose from, and food in my fridge to feed my hungry belly.

I am so grateful to work with such amazing people. These folks are passionate about the work they do, and they make a difference in many people's lives. I feel incredibly blessed to work with them and to feel inspired by each and every one of them.

I am thankful for my wonderful friend who recently allowed me to support and witness her deep struggles. I saw fear and pain in her eyes and was not able to do anything but stand in appreciation for this beautiful soul. I reached out and said, "I am here!" I was not able fix it, change it, or make it better, but I could sit and bear witness. For today, that has to be enough. To know another's struggle is a humbling experience.

I am grateful for a family who loves me dearly. I am thankful for the sun, the rain, the warm breeze, and the cold breeze. I am alive! I can feel it, experience it, and know it. This is my life! When the light shines bright or when the dark comes in, this is all mine to interpret and explore. Within each experience, I know the depths of my soul. Taking a moment throughout my day to ground myself in gratitude makes my life all the more rich. It reminds me to be thankful for what I have and to not lose sight of that in my pursuit for more. Taking the time to be grateful nurtures, enhances, and guides my desires as they emerge. I am so thankful for the strong foundation I exist on, and I am blending my passions and my heart's longing within my day-to-day experiences. My life is starting to look very much like *mine*!

Behind the Writing

I have gotten into the practice of giving thanks each morning as I get ready and each night just before bed. At first, I scheduled a reminder into my phone so I would not forget to do this activity. Now I find myself throughout the day giving thanks. It has become second nature to me, and I can feel my heart dance in delight each time I take the time to stop and be thankful for all I have. Take some time to journal on gratitude.

- List ten things you are most proud of accomplishing in the last year.
- List ten things from this past week.
- List three people you are grateful for and why.
- List three things from the day that you are thankful for.

- Consider the ways your gratitude contributes to your sense of understanding freedom.

As much as possible, try not to repeat an item, experience, or person on more than one list. Is this something you can add to your five-minute morning/evening routine?

I found a poem in a local newspaper many years ago, and I use it as a wonderful reminder of how blessed my life truly is. Consider adapting the below poem or create your own as a daily reminder.

> If you have food in your fridge, clothes on your back, a roof over your head and a place to sleep, you are richer than 75 percent of the world.
>
> If you have money in the bank, your wallet, and some spare change, you are among the top 8 percent of the worlds wealthy.
>
> If you woke up this morning with more health than illness, you are more blessed than the million people who will not survive this week.
>
> If you have never experienced the danger of battle, the agony of imprisonment or torture, or the horrible pangs of starvation, you are luckier than 500 million people alive and suffering.
>
> If you can read this message, you are more fortunate than 3 billion people in the world who cannot read it at all.
>
> —Author Unknown

Riding the Wave of Adventure

Today the sun was shining bright, the sky was blue, and the ocean was calling me. Adventure was patiently waiting for me to get the day started, and before my feet even hit the floor, my body was alive with excitement and anticipation.

I arrived at a surprisingly quiet beach two hours before my surf lesson. I was instantly aware of the sound of the powerful and magnificent waves as they crashed against the shore. I closed my eyes, feeling the warmth of the sun on my face, and I allowed the sound of the waves to hypnotize me, bringing a sense of peace and soothing to my being.

One hour before my lesson, my nerves kicked in. My tummy suddenly felt unsettled, and my mind started racing. *Maybe I should skip the lesson and just enjoy the quiet of the day. I wonder if there are sharks. Is it safe to surf if there are sharks?*

I knew I was going to surf that day, but yet my thoughts rambled on. For some reason today, I was aware of my mind chatter. Maybe it was the sun, the adventure, or my recent focus on my journey of self-discovery, but I actually found my thoughts entertaining. With that awareness, I reminded myself of how amazing I always feel after I face my fears.

I decided to take the time to quiet my mind. As I silenced the mind chatter and listened only to the sound of the waves, I could hear the ocean calling me and inviting me to play. From deep within, I started to feel the excitement stirring again as the anticipation of the adventure neared.

The adventure began, and I remembered my love of the ocean. I loved the feel of the board beneath my feet, the power of the wave as it took me for a ride, the stinging sensation as the ocean water got in my eyes, the sound of the wave crashing against my board, and the roaring thunder as I surrendered to the wave while it fully consumed me. At the end of the day, I felt completely exhausted and exhilarated.

From the day's adventure, I realized that these activities are like an active mediation for me. During my time on the board, I thought of nothing else but the task at hand: how I grasped the rails, how I popped up on the board, how I placed my feet depending on the board's nose, how I angled my body, and how I lowered my stance in order to gain power as I rode the edge of the wave. Each time I lost my balance, I embraced the experience of surrendering to the wave.

There was no to-do list running through my mind. I didn't think about bills I had to pay, tomorrow's class, or work worries. I didn't even think about my fear of sharks; I was fully present in the moment. So much so that when a beautiful four-foot baby shark swam under my board as I caught the edge of a wave, instead of fear, I felt deep appreciation, admiration, and acceptance of the experience. Adventure, my dear friend, you are a wonderful gift in my life. Thank you!

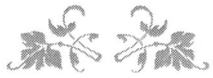

Behind the Writing

I am making it a practice to find adventure in each of my days. For me, adventure is another word for freedom. I have come to value the importance of adventure in my life on the weekends and throughout my days. An hour, a vacation, simple or big—if it makes my heart soar, then it adds value to my life. Take some time to journal:

- What does adventure mean to you?
- How can you add more adventure into your days/life?

Freedom, Vulnerability, and Love

- What relationship does adventure have with freedom for you?
- How can you add more of this to your life?

Recently I worked on an exercise called It Is Never as Bad as You Imagined It Could Be! Take some time to explore this exercise from scenarios of activities, adventures, or goals you would like to move forward on but have fear of. This exercise helps show that—in the vast majority of cases—the likelihood of disaster is far lower than we fear. Explore how fear is holding you back unnecessarily.

It Is Never as Bad as You Imagined It Could Be

What fears hold you back from reaching your goals and dreams? Take a situation, think of all the things that could go wrong, and write them down. Review your list to assess the likelihood of these things occurring. Explore what options, opportunities, or good could come from those occurrences. I have come to understand that more than 90 percent of our stress is stuff that will never happen. Fear causes us to lose a lot of time, energy, and experiences. It is important to understand the risk, but the next step is to put in place solutions/options/plans that help mitigate the risk(s), allowing you to move past the fear in order to reach your goals/desires.

Reframing My Story

There is so much power in the stories we tell ourselves. *Am I lost in this world? Am I just rediscovering the wonderful gifts of freedom, vulnerability, and love? Am I remembering the things I have always known? Is this my time to rediscover the essence of who I am? Am I just fooling myself? Am I in denial because none of this really matters anyway?* I have always understood the power of the stories we tell ourselves, but I am beginning to question my interpretation of some of my stories. At times, I wonder how to make sense of the world without the stories?

For many years, my story has been that I work hard and play harder. I can put Wonder Woman to shame; I am a supermom. I am independent and can do it all singlehandedly. I am not lucky in love. I am too deep, and that is overwhelming for others. In my constant pursuit of self-discovery, I exhaust anyone who chooses to partner with me. I am easy to fall in love with but hard to be in love with. I am fairly successful, and I have a good job, a nice home, food in the fridge, and change in my pocket. But none of these can capture the essence of who I really am.

When I was in my twenties, I witnessed a truck backing into a parking spot that already had a car in it. It was my first experience of understanding how powerful the mind was at creating a story in order to make sense of an experience. When the police arrived, they asked what I had witnessed. I explained my surprise that the driver did not see the parked car.

The officer suggested that there was no driver. I explained how I was sure I had seen a driver. The officer asked me to describe the driver, but I could not. After a few minutes of trying to wrack my brain, the officer let me off the hook and explained that there had been no driver. I attempted to explain that there had to have been a driver. The truck backed up and then turned on a ninety-degree angle into the parking spot. How could that happen without a driver? I was sure I had seen a driver!

The officer explained that the truck had popped into gear and rolled backward. It then hit a sewage drain, which turned the tires, but there had definitely not been a driver. Wow. The story my mind created to explain my experience had been so real that I could almost see a driver—a driver that never existed.

My journey over the last few months really helped me explore the different stories I tell myself. It gave me the opportunity to reframe many of them. For today, my new story is to decide each day when I wake up who I want to be that day. I get to build, choose, and witness the story from there! I am Kathy, and in my journey of self-discovery, I am becoming the creator of my stories!

Behind the Writing

On a day off from a conference I was attending, I decided to go to the beach to write. As I approached the bus stop, another family was already there waiting. An hour later, the family was visibly frustrated and upset that the bus had not yet come. At first, I wondered why they were so upset, and then I wondered why I was *not* upset. I quickly realized the difference was what we were choosing to focus on. There were two stories. My story was a warm sunny day with time to write, waiting on a bus that would soon take me to the beach. The other story was a wasted hour in the hot sun, waiting for a bus to arrive.

Opportunities such as this arise every day. Take the time to use these opportunities to practice reframing the story you tell yourself. The subconscious mind uses old behavior patterns in order to automatically respond and react to everyday life events. These learned responses and thought patterns enable us to automatically respond to circumstances, quickly and easily. Being aware is the first step in changing. One exercise that has helped me create awareness of my unsupportive thinking habits/stories is the No Complaining Exercise.

No Complaining Exercise

For one full day, do not allow yourself to complain (even within your thoughts). When you catch yourself complaining (and you will), gently correct and reframe the complaint into a more supportive thought. Changing the subconscious programming is a slow process that requires patience, but it is worth the time and effort. Remember to journal each day about your successes and areas for improvement with this exercise. Our thoughts can be the cage that traps us—or the key that frees us!

Vulnerability

Vulnerability is surrendering to experiences as they unfold, embracing your human emotions (and listening to their valuable messages), accepting that your thoughts make your experience good or bad, and knowing that the risk was worth it in the end!

Vulnerability

The juiciest possibilities often have the best disguises.
—Brené Brown

Vulnerability has been patiently waiting to meet me my entire life. It has knocked on my door many times. Each time, I have peeked out to say, "Sorry. No one is home. Try again another day."

There may have been the odd time when vulnerability knocked loud enough that I got curious and took a quick look. Maybe once or twice, we made eye contact, but each time, I quickly closed the door. Looking back now, I can see that I quite possibly could have won an Academy Award for best actress, playing the lead role of "Vulnerability." But Vulnerability always knew the truth, even when I did not; it was all just an act. I have spent most of my life trying to protect myself from the world. I have been trying to control the outcome(s), to know the answers before the questions were even asked, and to protect my heart by closing down and pushing away all that threatened to expose the truth. Vulnerability was not welcomed here.

This week, I opened the door just enough so that we could introduce ourselves. It was not an easy introduction. Staring into the eyes of Vulnerability, I saw into the depths of my soul. In doing so, I felt my soul ache, tear, nearly drown in sorrow, and cry out in a pain that I had never known. At the same time, I felt my soul open and felt the magic of inspiration, the delight of hope, the raging fire of desire, and the truth of love. In doing so, I experienced the delightful, juicy, enchanting experience of gaining just a bit more clarity into my life's purpose. It was a beautiful gift, and my soul enjoyed the dance even when the tears would not stop.

Vulnerability, thank you for your patience. Thank you for believing I would find my way. I am learning to be honest with myself, then others, and to not put on a brave face. I am learning to experience the freedom that comes when my soul dances in the delight of expressing who I am. I am learning to be in my sadness and to really feel it. I am learning to say, "Look at me, world. I am here. I am vulnerable. And in that vulnerability, I am finding my strength."

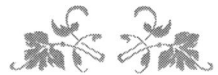

Behind the Writing

Vulnerability is the willingness to risk the hurt, the sadness, and the loss for all that is to be gained. At times, it means embracing the darkness in order to experience love, joy, and belonging. It is knowing and owning your life story—the good, the bad, the dark, the light—and moving from merely existing to really living!

Each of us has the privilege and the responsibility to design our own lives. Our daily habits and decisions create the foundations for the future. With this in mind, knowing what we truly want becomes incredibly important. For many of us, it is easy to get lost in the busyness of the day-to-day routine of life and lose sight of who we are and what makes our souls dance in delight. Dreaming of meeting our heart's longing, for many, can make us feel vulnerable. When we start to see that vulnerability is a great strength, and not a weakness, we are empowered with hope and the will to go for it! Take the time to explore these questions in your journal:

- Does vulnerability represent strength or weakness to you? Why or why not?
- When you were a child, what made you happiest?

- When you were a child, what did you want to be when you grew up?
- In the past ten years, what has stirred your soul?
- In the past year, what has stirred your soul?
- In the past week, what has stirred your soul?
- If money did not matter—and you knew you could not fail—what would you do over the next year?
- What daily practices do you need to put in place in order to create the tomorrow of your desires?
- Can you learn to be comfortable while living in a state of vulnerability?

Embracing the Language of the Heart

*The less you open your heart to others,
the more your heart suffers.*
—Deepak Chopra

For the vast majority of my life, I believed that emotions were a human weakness. For many years, my mantra was "Big girls don't cry." I actually praised myself for this, held it up as some sign to the world that I was strong, I was a survivor, and I could handle anything.

I was a doer, a mover, a shaker, and a high achiever. I had an A-plus personality. Emotions were a sign of weakness. I kept people far enough away to feel safe that no one—and no emotion—could ever bring me to my knees. I needed to be a pillar of strength for my parents, my brother, and my two daughters. To trust others with my heart was like opening Pandora's box.

When I look back and try to pinpoint the time when I decided to guard my heart from others, I sadly realize it has been a long time. High school was likely the turning point. In the first month of ninth grade, I went to my first house party. I was in awe of the experience, but I quickly learned that the cool tenth-grade girls had decided that they hated me without ever having uttered a word to me.

I spent the next few years wondering what I had done to them to bring on such hatred. It was a difficult time in my life. I figured out that if I kept to myself as much as possible, I was less likely to get hurt, disappointed, or harassed by others. Very few people could say they really knew me; I only trusted a few enough to give them a glimpse into who I really was. That was my world of understanding.

From an outsider's perspective, I still managed to be an overachiever and a doer. Years later, I bumped into a guy from high school who asked if university was hard to adjust to since I had gone from being so popular in high school to being a nobody at such a large university. From his perspective, I had been popular—the captain of the cheerleading squad, dating the quarterback of the football team, and so on. In hindsight, this odd conversation really illustrated how the wall I built around my heart made me always feel alone—despite how it appeared to others.

I loved university. I made friends who I could keep at a safe distance. I could go in and out of classes without much notice. My roommate/best friend once said she had never met anyone so monotone in her life. I had no real ups and no real downs. I just kept busy, and I liked it that way. I liked that I knew lots of people, but I didn't really know anyone—and they didn't know me.

I prided myself on being strong and pushing through, despite the odds and the bruises in life. I pushed through with my mind not my heart. The wall I built was so big and strong that knocking it down was impossible for anyone. The bricks around my heart were made in honor of my fear of humiliation, rejection, betrayal, sadness, and heartbreak. I actually convinced myself that it was in the name of strength.

In recent years, I started to remove the bricks, but just a few at a time. In the last few weeks, I shifted from removing one brick at a time to breaking down the walls around my heart with a drive and yearning I felt only a few times in my life. The journey of writing really helped me see that I wanted so much more out of life. I was hungry for the passion that was starting to stir from the depths of my soul.

I wanted to know my life from a place of vulnerability and mystery. My desire to really live my life to the fullest, heart opened, had been calling me for so long. I experienced many wonderful, amazing steps, but deciding to share this journey with you was like stepping out off the ledge. It was a leap of faith. In all my rawness, openness, and exposure, here I am—real and vulnerable.

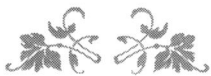

Behind the Writing

Our emotions are valuable tools for navigating our world. Our emotions tell us if what we are doing is aligned with what we desire. Emotions are the body's form of communication. Our emotions can signal the gap that exists between where/who we are and where/who we want to be. This is valuable information if we take the time to listen and understand the messages. The Feel Good Now Exercise has provided me with great practice in listening, understanding, and interpreting my emotions.

Feel Good Now Exercise

Notice how you feel? Do you feel discomfort, agitation, irritation, or sadness? Do you feel joy or happiness? Focus on what you can adjust or do in order to feel good now. By focusing on personal wellness and feeling good, you will slowly notice a change in the way you interpret your world. Create a mantra or self-talk statement that will help you change your thought focus from unsupportive to supportive. Two examples you might consider are "Each day my life gets better and better" or "In this moment, I desire to feel good."

As hard as it is to believe at times, how you feel is entirely up to you. In addition to this exercise, consider what other practices you have put in place or can put in place to support the idea of feeling good now.

- Get out in nature.
- See an osteopath, chiropractor, or a massage therapist.
- Explore alternative therapies such as Reiki, reflexology, or acupuncture.

- Do a detoxifying cleanse four times per year.
- Journal daily on how you are feeling throughout the day. Determine when and how your ego messages impact your feelings. Explore what you can do to feel good now.

Take some time to assess the daily habits you are putting in place. Which of these practices help you feel good? Consider changing, adjusting, or tweaking your daily practices with a focus on increasing your experience of feeling good.

Emotions—Embracing the Human Experience

You can't start the next chapter in your life
if you keep rereading the last one!
—Author unknown

I slowly walked through the house and packed boxes that represented the ending of one chapter and the beginning of a new one. I witnessed each emotion as it surfaced in my being, noticing that my current thoughts related to my physical task evoked different emotions.

I moved from anger to sadness and then joy as I touched something that brought a flood of memories. I watched my state of being move from tears of rage to tears of deep sorrow to tears of gratitude—all with a profound awareness of the overwhelming mix of emotions that washed over and through me.

As I packed the last of the boxes, I realized I was turning the page to start the next chapter of my life. With that thought, I experienced great joy, excitement, and a sense of adventure. Freedom and vulnerability gently whispered in my ear. With each new day, I was learning the delicate balance between the past, future, and the now. Each new day brought me closer to living my days filled with my passions.

During dinner that night, my daughters and I talked about what our lives might look like in a year. My girls were amazing; there were no barriers, blocks, or limits. We shared the desire to see our lives be happy and filled with love, travel, adventure, friends, and new beginnings. As we shared our stories about our bright futures, I was aware of how my spirit soared and my desires deepened. To my surprise, I was smiling. Refreshing and exhilarating laughter wrapped us in a warm hug.

I embraced my human experience of emotions and the dance with each one brought forward that day. My emotions took me for a ride—some I would rather not have been on and others I would have loved to stay on for a lifetime. The new chapter I am about to start is exciting, scary, and sometimes overwhelming. I am filled with deep gratitude for all of it. I would rather embrace the dance than sit it out. I know I am better off for it.

Behind the Writing

Our emotions hold important information that helps us determine where we are in relationship to where we want to be. Take some time to explore the valuable messages your emotions showed you today. Did you seek to understand the messages—or did you simply react? How can you take notice of these messages in order to manage yourself in ways that benefit you? Understanding the messages that our emotions bring is not always easy. Patience and daily journaling can provide great insight.

Hide-and-Seek with Happiness

As a young child, happiness invited me to play hide-and-seek, and I was it. The game played out for most of my life. It seemed that each time I found happiness, it decided it was time to play again. Disappearing again, leaving me to continue the search. I have come to realize that it has been my *idea* of happiness that has eluded me for years.

As a young teenager, I looked up at the stars at night and wished to be happy. I spent many of my teen years feeling great sadness. I never understood why. I actually felt guilty for it because I had two parents who loved me dearly, a nice home, and camping trips every second summer. I had food in my belly, an enjoyable part-time job, and a few good friends who really cared about me.

My expectations often left me feeling disappointed. I read way too many romance novels, saw way too many Hollywood movies, and bought into the whole idea that happiness would arrive in a package with a pretty little bow. I had high expectations for myself, and things never turned out as I thought they would. Even if the outcome was fantastic, there was still a sense of "less than" because I was so attached to what it was "supposed" to look like.

Self-judgment and self-criticism were also thieves in the plot to rob me of my happiness. For way too long, they did just that in my life. For most of my life, I felt I was not good enough. I was always criticizing myself and expecting more of myself. Even today, I have to be careful.

I make my to-do lists far greater than is physically possible, and I am disappointed at the end of the day when I have not crossed off every item.

During a phone call with my amazing and wonderful peer coach, Laurie reminded me that my goals for the week were unrealistic and undoable. She noticed my pattern of ending the week disappointed that I had not gotten everything done—instead of seeing all that I had gotten done. As obvious as it was to others, it was something that had eluded me for most of my life.

When I stay present in the moment, without expectations or attachments to a specific outcome, happiness flows throughout my being. This is still a practice; I have many years of habits to reprogram. When I find myself irritated, frustrated, or uneasy, I focus my intentions on my breath. Breathing in and out, knowing I am loved, and knowing I love, are the important things. When I bring myself back to the thoughts of all that is truly important, I feel peace growing from within. You cannot *have* happiness; you can only *be* happiness.

> "Letting go gives us freedom, and freedom is the
> only condition for happiness. If, in our hearts,
> we still cling to anything—anger, anxiety,
> or possessions—we cannot be free."
> —Thich Nhat Hanh

Behind the Writing

Reprograming your habits is essential to living your life differently. The subconscious mind requires repetition of new patterns, habits, and thoughts in order to change. This includes being aware of the messages we receive from those we spend the most time with.

I have come to understand the importance of who I surround myself with. I have made a considerable effort over the past few months to

Freedom, Vulnerability, and Love

reach out to those around me who are passionate about what they do in their lives. This helps keep me focused on my goals, desires, and my life purpose.

Take some time to explore whether the books, people, and activities you surround yourself with are supportive or unsupportive to your life. Consider the following questions:

- Who are the five people you are closest with? Is your exposure to these individuals helping you or holding you back?
- Who do you spend the most time with? Is this exposure helping or holding you back?
- Who on this list is the most influential person in your life? Why?
- What are the last five books you read?
- Who are your role models? Consider who and why?
- What movies are you watching? Do these provide supportive messaging or unsupportive?
- From your answers above what daily habits do you need to stop? Increase? Remove?
- As you start to get more in touch with the messages from your heart, do you feel vulnerable? And if so do you see this as a good thing? Why or why not?

Anger from Deep Within

Anger came into my life, kicking and screaming, despite my attempts to quiet, silence, and ignore it. I did not like the knot in my stomach, the sweaty palms, or the sound of rushing water in my ears; they were sure signs that anger was erupting from deep within.

I had spent a good portion of my life working really hard not to feel anger. I acted as if I had power over such an emotion. I have learned to slow my speech down and to pay extra attention to ensure that my voice does not rise when anger visits. I have learned to remove myself from situations as fast as I can if I suspect anger is bubbling within, but I am not nearly as good at this as I wish I was.

For many years, I told myself that I was less than if I felt anger toward another. If anger was allowed to visit, it was a sign that my mind was weak. In recent years, I have read many books about emotional intelligence in my attempts to understand anger as a signal that something was not right, a source of information rather than a weakness.

In the past, my mind was good at creating stories that denied my physical and emotional reactions. It was as if my body and my mind battled to see who was really in control; at a first glance, it appeared that the mind typically won.

Today, something came up that was difficult for me. I was blindsided by my body's immediate response of overwhelming anger. Like an observer of my own experience, I watched my mind try to deny and rationalize the feelings of anger. I said, "I trust everything will work out as it is supposed to. It is not my place to judge another. What is meant to be will be. My job is to do the best that I can." None of these true statements rationalized my body's experience of anger.

Instead of trying to hide it, fix it, or self-talk myself into denying it, I sat with the anger. I respectfully spoke my anger. I dug deep to know what was behind my anger. I listened to the message anger was bringing me. What was I afraid of? What was mine to own? How could I handle things differently next time? How was I going to manage this? I moved through my experiences while honoring my mind and my emotions, recognizing the extreme value that both offer my life.

Behind the Writing

Anger can serve as a signal that something important is going on. Anger is neither good nor bad. Take some time to journal and explore the questions below. Use your anger as a tool to provide you with valuable information about what is working and what is not working in your life.

- What does anger look like in you?
- When you feel angry, do you feel vulnerable? Do you see this vulnerability as a strength or a weakness?
- Can you feel it before it surfaces? What are the early internal signals that your anger is bubbling?
- Witnessing an emotion and acting out in that emotion are two different things. What strategies can you put in place to honor the valuable message anger is bringing you without acting out the behavior of anger? How can you manage your behaviors in ways that are supportive?

Consider these questions while replacing anger with fear, frustration, etc. Explore getting to know all your emotions and the behaviors that typically accompany those emotions. Journal about your daily experiences as you become more aware of your emotions and identify your accompanying behaviors. With greater awareness, you will be able to honor your emotions while behaving in ways that are aligned with your desired outcomes.

From the Darkness, There Is Peace

Lately, change felt like an unexpected houseguest who was getting far too comfortable and at home in my life. I found myself wondering what the length of stay would be this time and hoped a departure date would arrive soon.

I knew change was a fact of life. I knew the transition time was moving me from one experience to another. I knew that change was often positive in my life. As hard as I tried to think my way into welcoming and celebrating the change, it still left me feeling uncomfortable at times.

I want to be comfortable and laid back when it comes to changes and transitions in my life. I keep reading that a shared characteristic of successful people is their ability to adapt to change; it is a sign of modern-day intelligence. I want to master this ability but recognize I have a lot of practice ahead of me.

For months, I had been experiencing little changes, big changes, and even bigger changes. I was waiting for closure on some things and for new beginnings on others. The transition time has been difficult and has weighed on me at times. I was far more stressed than I even wanted to acknowledge. I was working hard to find peace within the stress. I wondered if working so hard to make peace within was making things more stressful.

I told myself that I loved the transition time, but I was still faking it until I made it. I told myself that I was not stressed, but my telltale signs showed differently. Over the years, I learned many useful self-care techniques that I utilized during that transition time. I went to the climbing gym a minimum of two times per week. I tried to get out for one good hike a week, using the time to creatively paint with light in photos. I saw my massage therapist and my osteopath on a regular basis.

For two months straight, I added meditation to my daily practice. Every morning, upon waking, I set my intention to see my world through my heart. As a result, I reached out and connected with some amazing people, and many of those relationships deepened with each new day. I danced in the kitchen as I attempted to pull a dinner together, and I made sure I spent quality time with my beautiful girls.

I wondered if I was actually doing myself a disservice by telling myself how much I loved the changes. Did I need a balance between the two? On Facebook, Twitter, and Instagram, I saw quotes on a daily basis that talked of looking forward, staying positive, and not paying attention to the shadows. What if by denying the shadow I am actually just pushing it out of my mind and denying what is in my body? I am coming to appreciate that my body and emotions provide me with important messages during stressful times.

When I was driving home alone, well into the darkness of the night, it started to snow. Big fluffy snowflakes gently fell from the darkness. Almost instantly, everything was covered in a soft blanket of white. As I pulled in the driveway, I immediately saw my loyal furry friend peering out at me from the front window in excitement. I stood in the dark, and the snow fell softly on my face, gently sticking to my eyelashes.

I closed my eyes, and the snow melted as it hit my skin. Being fully present in the moment, I heard—deep from within—wonder, freedom, vulnerability, and the overwhelming sensation of love as it surrounded me. They were almost like my own personal support group. From the darkness, there was peace. My entire body felt a sense of ease and flow and sent me a message of hope and acceptance.

Change, you are here again in my life. We are not yet friends, but with each passing day, I am learning to understand you. I am gaining an appreciation for the gifts you bring my life. Maybe that is enough for today. Today I celebrate that I have an excellent self-care plan. The signs of stress are there to serve as a reminder to stay awake and stay present in the moment. There is a lot to learn from this experience. As I walk through the front door, I count all my blessings and wonder if one day I might actually thrive in change. Now that would be something!

Behind the Writing

Change is often accompanied by feelings of vulnerability. When we view vulnerability and/or change as negative and become resistant or fearful, the experience is often much harder on us than it needs to be. Change is going to happen to us all several times throughout our lives. I highly recommend that you watched the incredible TEDx talk about vulnerability by Brené Brown. It is truly enlightening and will help you explore the beautiful gifts vulnerability can bring to your life on a deeper level.

I have also found it beneficial to develop strategies for dealing with the stresses that often accompany the changes in my life. I particularly like visualization exercises. Visualization can be a form of meditation or a form of learning/practicing control over our thoughts. Many athletes use it to perfect their skills by envisioning the perfect pitch, the perfect basket, etc.

When I was young, I used visualizations to fall asleep. Sadly, I chose to visualize such stories such as *Romeo and Juliet*, which I am sure further complicated my understanding of love. Nonetheless, it strengthened my skills in visualization meditations. When I feel stressed now, I use this technique. With practice, it can become a powerful tool for managing stress in your life.

You can use a guided visualization meditation or create your own. The Happy Place Visualization Exercise is a fairly easy personalized meditation.

Happy Place Visualization Meditation Exercise

Simply create a picture in your mind of the ideal place of rest and peace. What does it look like? What colors do you see? What does it feel like? Touch things in your mind's eye. Explore the texture of each new thing you discover. What sounds do you hear? Can you feel the sun and wind? What can you smell? What can you taste? The more detail you use, the deeper and more beneficial the meditation will be.

Consider adding a visualization meditation to your five-minute morning routine as a great way to start your day. Take some time to journal and capture any realizations you have that come from the experience of visualizing.

Vulnerability Wants to Play

O   h no. There it is again. The door is knocking, louder and louder. I pulled the blankets over my head and whispered, "No, not today. I am too tired, too worn down. Please not today."

The knocking got louder and louder. I felt it vibrating throughout my being. Vulnerability wanted in and was not going to take no for an answer. Vulnerability had touched my soul, and my soul now refused to live without it. Slowly, I got up and answered the door.

Vulnerability said, "Can you play today?"

I answered, "Yes. Yes. Yes!"

In honor of Freedom and Vulnerability, I decided to take a risk and share many things about myself that few people know:

- I sleep with my eyes partially open. Some people may think that is weird. Yes, it is possible—despite the fact that I once had an eye doctor who did not believe me. It has been confirmed that I do sleep with my eyes partially open. When I was a teenager, I actually searched to see if there was a cure. I looked into hypnosis, surgery, anything to rid me of this weirdness. When I was traveling across Europe in my twenties, I found a temporary solution. I pulled a baseball cap down over my eyes or wrapped a jacket around my head. In more recent years, I have made peace with this.
- I have traveled to more than thirty-five countries, and although I have only been to Ireland twice, it feels like home.

- I was diagnosed with a learning disability as a kid and bought that crap until recently when I discovered how much I love writing. Likely, these struggles made me stronger, and few people know how terrible I am at spelling thanks to spell-check.
- I love doing photo shoots despite my awkwardness. It makes me feel sexy!
- When delivering my firstborn, my body went into crisis. I had fever, convulsions, pain-blindness (my eyes worked, but I could not see a thing), and situational delusions. I also had a conversation with God. I tried to explain that his decision to make woman suffer in labor was unfair just because Eve bit the forbidden fruit. I made my husband (at the time) swear never to speak of this; to my knowledge, he never has.
- When I laugh really hard, which is not nearly as often as I would like, I squeal like a piglet. The sounds only make me laugh harder, resulting in louder piglet squeals, streams of tears, and aching sides.
- I judge myself constantly. I am incredibly hard on myself.
- I rarely ever drink and just recently discovered why. One of my pain values is loss of control. Since drinking makes me feel a loss of control, it scares me.
- My girls and I have a rule of no jumping on the beds at home, but we must jump on the beds every time we stay in a hotel.
- I am secretly jealous that my parents are so artistic—and I am not.
- I took salsa and Lindy Hop dance lessons for two years. And even after all that time, I still struggled with letting someone else lead. But I love to dance!
- I sang karaoke once. It was a ton of fun! I trembled with fear the entire time and was really bad at it.
- I am terrible at remembering names.
- What I love the most about the extreme sports I participate in is that they scare the hell out of me, but I do them anyway. In that moment of pushing past the fear, I experience some of the most exhilarating and freeing moments in my life. I am learning

to do that in my everyday moments. I am learning that when I look fear in the face and go for it, I have great clarity, insight, depth, passion, and pure joy.

I am learning that Vulnerability and I are becoming dear friends.

Behind the Writing

I posted this writing on my blog. At first, I was absolutely terrified that I was sharing a number of fairly embarrassing things about myself with the world. To my surprise, putting this out there really had a freeing impact on me. Somehow, what once felt embarrassing no longer seemed all that important.

Make it a practice to do at least one thing a week that scares you. Embrace your vulnerability—and walk through your fears. Each week, you will feel more and more empowered. What can you do today? If you would like to explore these ideas in greater detail or if you are struggling to implement any of these strategies, book a complementary session with me to determine how I may further support and serve you – www.kathybazinet.com (coaching)

Love

*Fear and love cannot exist in the same moment.
And you get to choose which one you experience.*

Just Breathe

I decided to put down my weapons of war and try a new tactic with the battle that rages within me and the enemy I have known as ego.

As I drove to work today, I felt carefree. I was smiling, a melody was escaping my lips, and a warm fall breeze was blowing through my hair. I was not aware of any thoughts; I was lost in the task of driving.

Ego chose that moment for a surprise attack. "What is there to smile about? You are all alone in this world. Your driving destination is another long, boring meeting that never really accomplishes anything. You don't even know your life's purpose."

The smile left my face, my insides tossed and turned, and I remembered the familiar feeling of being lost. That day, from somewhere deep within me, I heard a gentle reminder to "just breathe."

My ego's negative self-talk threw me off. The stories I invent in my head can turn from adventures into the mystery of the unknown to dark plots and sinister characters involved in my most recent life drama. I have been battling less with ego and am learning to slowly and cautiously consider becoming friends. Maybe instead of fighting with ego, I can learn to appreciate the gifts ego provides in my life. Ego has served me well on many occasions. With each new day, I am gaining an understanding of how powerful my thoughts are. I am learning to shift them from fear to appreciation and gratitude. Instead of judging and criticizing myself, I am focusing on manifesting my heart's desires and taking responsibility for my thoughts.

With each new day—and each new discovery of who I am and what I want—I start to turn the story around. I start to feel excitement in what the future holds, what adventures are here now, and what more are to come. I start to remember that the greatest gift I can give myself is the love of self, and that brings acceptance, forgiveness, and less pressure. The key is to change the old story to a new one that is supportive. When I feel overwhelmed, as if I have failed again, or that life is really hard, I remember that I don't need to listen to my ego. In that moment, there is nothing I need to do except breathe. I am whole. I am enough!

Behind the Writing

Take time out every day to love and nurture yourself. I have made a considerable effort to make friends with my breathing. It is important to recognize the power of your breath and its ability to calm the body. Consider one or both of the breathing exercises.

Self-Hypnosis Exercise

This simple exercise is a form of self-hypnosis. Breathe in while counting to twenty. Then hold your breath to a count of forty. As you exhale, visualize or hear your inner voice saying your name. My experience with this technique has been incredible relaxation.

Visualization Exercise

Take a deep breath while visualizing the number fifty. As you exhale, hold the image of the number fifty in your mind's eye, and using your inner voice, say, "Relax." Visualize each number in detail and hold the image in your mind for a minimum of ten seconds before moving to the next number. Continue this while you count down. This is not as easy as it sounds. Your mind might wander off before you are far into the counting. Gently bring yourself back to counting where you left off. In time, you will improve in keeping the focus, and your body will respond to the relaxation command much faster.

Take some time to journal the experience with the breathing exercises. How can you add them to your daily practice?

The Gift of Love

Learning to live with my heart open was not always easy for me. I have always been a thinker; my mind does not quiet very often. With all that mind chatter, it was difficult to actually hear the whispers of the heart. The result is that very few people have found a home in my heart. When you try to "think" your way through life, it is easiest to keep people at a safe distance. In my journey of self-discovery, over the last few months, I have been learning to quiet my mind. Slowly, my heart has been coming alive.

Please do not misunderstand me. I have a deep loving and engaged relationship with my two amazing children. I love my family, and I cherish my friends, but there have been few times when even those closest to me have seen the rare, exposed, heart-open Kathy. For a lot of my life, I have not known that side of myself. I have always preferred to be a fly on the wall, unnoticed and the onlooker. I have always enjoyed large crowds so I can blend into the background. I have excused this as my preference to be an observer rather than a participator.

To many people, I appear to be an open book. I can ramble on about my recent adventures or guide the conversation into a philosophical discussion where the depth of my insecurity, doubt, self-criticism, shame, guilt, and fear remain hidden from those around me. For the most part, this includes me.

Recently, I went on a humanitarian mission trip to Kenya with my dad and my eldest daughter. There were times when it was almost overwhelming for me. Although my written words can not do justice to the experience, here is my brief note:

Early in the trip, we visited a school for girls. Each one wanted to hug me, hold my hand, and show me the school and all they were learning. There was so much pride in their beautiful dark eyes. On one occasion, four young girls shoved each other in attempts to ask me questions. I felt awkward, unsure, and uneasy. My mind raced with thoughts of how to get the attention off of me. It was supposed to be about them. It was their time to shine, but they wanted me to feel special, welcomed, and cared for.

As the time went by, this experience occurred over and over again. On our last day while visiting the school, I asked, "What do you do if you want alone time?"

The girls looked confused. No one knew how to answer me. It quickly became obvious that this was a foreign concept to them.

The girls started giggling. One beautiful soul asked, "Why would someone want to be alone?"

I could not answer their question. I struggled to explain why to myself. I felt a young girl's hand take mine; another sweet young girl grabbed me and hugged me. To my surprise, I melted into their embraces. I was forever changed. It was so overwhelming that at the time I could not understand it; the way I experience my world had started to change.

Weeks later, now back at home, I attended the We Day event, which was hosted by the organizations we traveled to Kenya with—Me to We—Free the Children (two organizations that work together in their efforts to eliminate worldwide child slavery while at the same time empowering the youth to "be the change"). When the Kenyan Boys Choir came out on stage and sang Bob Marley's "One Love," tears started to stream down my face. That was the gift that Kenya gave me. The change was so profound. My heart was opening, and I was learning to see my world from my heart.

I am starting to learn how to silence the voice within that tells me I am not good enough—or that I am not worthy of love. I am learning to see beauty and love in the simplest of my experiences. I am slowly learning to look at the person in the mirror and whisper, "I love you."

Behind the Writing

I have always volunteered and tried to give back as much as possible in my life. I highly recommend humanitarian work for anyone who might be interested in it. It was an incredible feeling to be able to provide such support. When I give my love, I receive more love.

Consider where and when in your life you can give—time, money, or things. For example, at the beginning of each year, my girls and I plan our donation amounts and decide which organizations we will contribute to. Before Christmas and birthdays, we go through our closets to ensure we "give" in appreciation for what we are about to receive. We take the time to research the organizations we are giving to in order to ensure that our donations go to organizations that are in line with our family values.

In addition to giving, it is important to be a good receiver. In recent years, I have worked hard to also become a good receiver. When a woman I befriended at a conference generously offered me her spot at a publishing seminar after she read my blog, I graciously accepted. My ego had a field day with it. *Who am I to accept such a thing? That was too generous of her. How can I possibly repay her for this? I need to find a way to repay her.*

In the end, I e-mailed a note to say how grateful I was that she believed in me/my writing and how generous she had been. It feels great to give and wonderful to receive. Consider the following questions in your journal notes:

- How do you feel when you are giving/receiving?
- What self-love messages do you give yourself when you give?
- What self-love messages can you give yourself when you receive?

- In what ways do you already give (money, time, clothes, etc.)?
- How can you create more opportunities to experience giving and receiving? Consider how giving and receiving is a reflection of your self-love.

The Power of Believing and Loving Your Life

In the fall of 2012, I was preparing for an upcoming trip to Europe. I made the conscious decision to play with the idea of the power of manifestation. I had read many books, watched videos and movies, and attended many conferences about the law of attraction. As I boarded the plane, I stated that this would be the first of many trips in the upcoming year. Just dreaming of it excited me.

In the past, I would have rationalized this desire. *I have two amazing girls. How will I travel when they are both in school? How will I afford the cost of such travel? How will I get the time off work for such travel?* Instead, I decided to follow the rules of the law of attraction and not attach to any outcome or have any desire to figure out how it would all come about. I just trusted. I figured I had nothing to lose by dreaming while I was on a plane toward a European adventure.

By the end of November 2013, my travels included my first trip to France, Belgium, and the Netherlands, six separate trips to New Brunswick (three separate weeks and three weekends), a long weekend in Florida, two conferences in California; a humanitarian trip to Kenya with my father and eldest daughter, and Vancouver for a weeklong personal development boot camp. I took twelve trips in thirteen months.

I ended the year with amazement and gratitude for all the incredible travel opportunities during that year. My heart soared in delight with each experience, and I gained a greater appreciation and understanding of the importance of setting and stating my intentions. I believe that what I focus on is what I make my reality. This past year has shown me the value and, at times, the heartbreaking consequences of this power. From now on, I will respect and use caution when I clearly state what I desire.

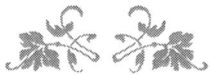

Behind the Writing

I believe that our daily practices and our thoughts create the foundations of our dreams. Review your vision board. Have any of your dreams or desires for your future changed? If so, adjust your vision board or make another one. Take the time to create goals for each of the dreams on your vision board. Decide what daily activities or tasks need to happen in order to reach your goals. Make this a quarterly practice.

I Love You!

It felt like I had longed for you for a lifetime. I wanted to know you, feel you, and have you touch my presence and consume all that I am. I waited for my soul to sing in delight as it reminded me of this familiar knowing that I somehow forgot. You were distant, withdrawn, and unknown, but I saw you. I caught slight glimpses and brief sightings of you, my authentic self, my passions, my desires, my heart's longings, and my love of self!

My new path had stirred my passion from within and awakened my soul to dance in the joy. My ego smiled in surprise. You were emerging from the darkness. It was quite unexpected, but those early glimpses began evolving. With each day, there was more clarity, a deeper understanding, and a knowing that was surfacing from the forgotten.

There have been times when I have wondered if I had known those discoveries would change my life in such profound ways, would I have ventured down that path? Ego whispers, "No way. Your life was pretty good the way it was. The losses have been too great. If you could turn back the clock, you would."

Today, I say, "Thank you, Ego, for so desperately wanting to protect me. I acknowledge that your protection has served me well at times—but not today. There is little I would change. I have no regrets. Learning to live my life differently will still have low times, great struggles, many tough decisions, and a whole lot of fear, but in the end, I know it is worth it all. I am worth it! With each new discovery, I feel more aligned with living my truth, my passions, and my purpose. This is who I am meant to be.

I still have so much work to do, but the work feels less and less like work—and more and more like living, loving, and being. On the surface, my life seems to have changed so little, but the space is being made on the inside. I am seeing life differently. I am discovering self-love, and I am forever changed. Each day I wake, I am more of the person I want to be.

Behind the Writing

Discovering my love of writing has been an incredible gift for me. It adds richness to my days. I might have a long day at my paid job, but knowing I will get in some writing time later that night makes my days richer. I have stopped making excuses that I do not have enough time in my days. Finding and doing the things I love has changed my life significantly. Take some time to explore the following questions:

- What is your passion?
- How can you breathe passion into everything you do?
- How can you incorporate your passion into every day?

For a number of weeks now I have been listening to Esther Hicks—Abraham (author and public speaker for Abraham Hicks teaching) on YouTube, on the topic of love. I am coming to understand the importance of seeing my world through the eyes of love rather than a desire to be loved. As I get ready in the morning, I take a moment to stare deep into my own eyes (while looking in the mirror) and gently say, "I love you, Kathy."

It was a difficult exercise in the beginning, but it gets much easier. A few weeks later, I can feel the love flow. There have been mornings when I have been moved to tears just by my own words of love being directed back to me.

Give this exercise a try. How does it make you feel? Note how you felt the first time you did the exercise and compare your notes after ten days. Has it gotten easier? What emotions come to the surface as you explore your own self-love? How does focusing on loving—rather than being loved—change your understanding of your world and of love?

Always Meant to Be

My new relationship with freedom and vulnerability stirs the desires and passions from within me. It makes the moments of my days juicier and richer. I long for this deeper understanding of who I am in every new experience I have. There are also days when my newfound relationship with vulnerability leaves me feeling raw, exposed, and open. On those days, I question—and even fear—whether I am now fragile.

My ability to turn my back on freedom and vulnerability has diminished. The once sturdy, reliable brick wall around my heart is now crushed rubble beneath my feet. At times, I feel so close to the edge; it is as if my world has been turned upside down. I wonder how easy it would be to knock me over. There are days when the path is no longer clear because living in a state of openness requires the compass to be set on a destination, but there is no longer a cleared path. Most days, this excites me, but there are moments and even days when I miss "thinking" I knew the next step, the next move, or that I had any real control over any of it.

This thought takes my breath away with excitement, but it also takes my breath away in fear. From where I stand, I see so many different paths around me, thousands of them actually. Where did they all come from? Just a short time ago, I knew one path, one destination, and one future plan. Now the options, opportunities, and choices are countless.

The exercise I am working on for today is to dream of what I want my future to be. What does it look like and include? What potential does it hold for me? What new path can I take? Who will I be if I dare to take that path? This exercise has no room for judgment (getting more specific will come later); it is just about the dream. I will give myself one month to add to each dream path and create more. After that, I will look closer at each path to see which is calling me.

Even though I feel vulnerable and fragile at times, I am likely the strongest I have ever been. I am taking the time to discover who I am—to explore, create, and design what I want my future to look like. It is more empowering than sitting back and watching it fall into place. I am still aware that life might bring about experiences that I do not favor—and that bad things do happen to good people. However, the more I know myself, and the more I design my own path, the closer I am to being the unique, genuine, and authentic me who I was always meant to be!

Behind the Writing

I have really come to appreciate the importance of knowing myself. When I reflect on the times I have gotten off track, I realize the common denominator has been that I forgot what I stood for. I found that other people's opinions and desires became my own when I was not being true to myself. Journaling helps keep me focused on my own needs, desires, and dreams. I discovered that it can be difficult to discern if I am being guided by my fear(s) or not. The Ask Your Friends Exercise is an excellent tool for gaining perspective.

Ask Your Friends Exercise

Reach out to six people you trust. They should know you fairly well and be able to provide you with an honest reflection of where you are in life (from their perspective). Ask them to answer the following questions:

- What do you think I have passions for and why?
- What do you think/know I stand for?
- What are my greatest natural strengths?
- If I wasn't doing what I am currently doing, what have you always thought I would be great at? A hobby? Volunteer work? A new career?

Before reviewing their responses, write down your answers to the same questions. When you review their responses, take some time to write what is consistent in them. What differs in the responses? Is your perspective of yourself similar to their perspectives of you? What insights can you learn from their answers and this exercise? What is one action step you will take today as a result of what you have just discovered?

For a Moment, I Was Lost in Wonderland

Wonder, you have been taunting me my entire life. Come play with me! Look into the rabbit hole; this is where the magic happens. Passion, purpose, and desire exist here. Come and look a little deeper. You have only just begun to scratch the surface.

I felt so awake and raw as I opened myself to the wonders of the world. I walked slower than usual into my office as Wonder invited me to awaken in this moment.

I was delighted when I noticed a small patch of grass that had been turned into a canvas painted with the vibrant red colors of fall leaves mingled with the wrinkled, dried brown leaves that had already completed their life cycles. Mixed among the leaves, fresh dew on the green grass sparkled in the early morning sunlight. There were water droplets along the blades. Excitement stirred within me as I stopped to play with the sunlight and captured this beauty in a photo.

As I walked along, I noticed shriveled slices of watermelon. I was curious about why they were along the edge of a garden. I took a moment and allowed myself to wonder about all the possible stories. I smiled when I thought of infinite possibilities I had not even yet considered, and I knew that none of the stories mattered. All that mattered was that moment, looking at those pieces of watermelon and smiling at the magical stories that emerged in my thoughts. Maybe I had watched *Alice in Wonderland* one too many times or maybe I would watch it again later that night.

I was drawn to the beautiful sound of the cardinal flying overhead and noticed the direct contrast between the bird's song and a passing gas-guzzling bus. I paused for a moment, closed my eyes, and listened as the two sounds blended into a unique song that I was certain was being created just for me.

I became aware of the warm sun on my face, the cool fall breeze that moved gently past me, and the sound of the leaves in the trees above as they gently danced down to my feet. I smiled as I wondered who else had been kissed by the sun and nibbled by the wind.

When I crossed a busy street, I became aware of the smell of gas as another bus passed by. The smell was strong and unpleasant, so I decided to stop to smell the flowers that were blooming just outside my office. This new smell brought forth a beautiful, cherished memory that had been long forgotten. I wondered in delight at how quickly the smell awoke the sense of adventure in me.

I felt as though I was being invited to play with wonder for just a bit longer. The door to my office building felt much heavier than I remembered it to be. It was as if the outside world was calling me to continue to dance with it. Instead, a young gentleman saw me struggle with the door and hurried over to help me. In that moment, I made eye contact with him—a perfect stranger—and felt an incredible sense of gratitude for his help. In that moment, I felt a connection to another soul and smiled.

It was a magical walk to work. I had done that ten-minute walk hundreds of times, but none had ever felt so delightful. With excitement and anticipation I wondered what the walk to my car at the end of the day would bring.

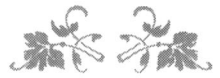

Behind the Writing

I have always loved being in the great outdoors, but quiet time in the woods has recently awakened my creativity. It has opened me up to the wonders of the world. A few weeks earlier, I had wrapped myself in a blanket and brought my laptop on a hike into the woods. I curled up under a tree and wrote and wrote. I felt so alive, so refreshed, and so excited. I took the time to play with the light as I photographed the beautiful colors around me. The time alone in nature really helped me connect deep within myself and allowed me to see the wonder and beauty of the world.

Consider spending some time in nature. Do you feel refreshed? Inspired? Motivated? If not nature, where can you go to stir your creativity? What takes you out of the normalcy of your day-to-day activities? What awakens your senses? Getting out and doing different things can help change your perspective and provide a fresh look at life. Finding ways to play in the wonder and joy of life is the essence of self-love. What can you do today to awaken your sense of wonder?

Standing Close to the Edge

As I leaned over the side of a cliff after a long hike deep in the woods, my hiking partner asked why I liked to stand so close to the edge. At the time, I did not have words that could answer that. I was also challenged about why I liked to skydive and asked to consider what it would take to get me to realize that I didn't need to take such big risks to really enjoy life.

At the time, it made me stop and think. I asked myself why I chose such adventures. No matter what answer I gave, the person pushed harder. Since I could not find the right words, I started to wonder why I needed such things. I wondered if my adventures gave me a false sense of freedom or a false sense of joy. I questioned myself for a long time. Now, a few years later, I know the answer.

I like to stand close to the edge, experience risk, adventure, and step outside the box of perceived safety because I can see a whole new world from that place! It's not about risking my life, being reckless, or even looking danger in the face. Danger is a real thing and is something to be avoided, but fear of the edge is just fear. I have learned how to get past the fear when I jump from the door of an airplane or when the waves hit me in the face and take my breath away just seconds before I descend on a dive. I have learned to move past fear as I climb into the raft for an afternoon of waves, rocks, and paddles, but finding a way to experience that freedom from fear in my day-to-day life can be difficult. I fear what others might think of me—and what I think of me. At times, I fear that I am not good enough.

I lost my way by believing that the edge could only be found at the doorway of the plane, at the bottom of the ocean, or hidden deep beneath my next adventure. I've learned that mistakes are a gift of learning and hard times are a gift of clarity. When I dare to be awake and really see, feel, and embrace everything around me, I am standing on the edge without any fear.

I do not get to decide if or when I'm going to die, but I *do* get to decide how I want to live. Lately, I have been exploring myself within. Can I be stronger, kinder, or more compassionate? Can I embrace freedom? Vulnerability? Love? Can I fully embrace my life? Can I breathe in the joy? I don't want to just survive the storm; what happens if I get to the other side and there is nothing left? I want to stand close to the edge, stare down the rabbit hole, and embrace all that life has to offer. Life seems to get sweeter with each new discovery.

Behind the Writing

When I do the things I love, it does not feel like work. It makes all the other things in my life even sweeter. For a long time, I forgot what I loved, what made my heart sing, and what put a smile on my face. I got busy in the normalcy of day-to-day living. I was existing instead of fully living. I want everyone to truly live the life they were meant live, to enjoy each and every day, and to allow the present moment to be rich with joy. Take a moment to reflect on your life.

- Are you doing the things you love the most?
- Are you smiling most days?
- What does standing close to the edge look like for you?
- What dreams do you have that are still unfulfilled?

Freedom, Vulnerability, and Love

- What is holding you back? How can you minimize the gap between your dreams and where you are now?
- What is one thing you can do today to further explore your life on a deeper level?

The Journey Continues

I will live each day of this journey so at the end of this life, I will be able to say, "It was a hell of a ride!"

Living Life Fully

If today were my last day on earth, would I consider my life to have been successfully mine or tragically lived based on others' expectations/rules/opinions? I think there have been times when I have had my head down and blindly followed the rules and expectations. There were times I sat back and watched as the path formed in front of me because I did not seek to understand what I truly wanted for my life. There have been other times when my life has truly been all mine: freeing, magnificent, and filled with awe. At other times, I brought the darkness upon myself and became lost in that empty space. But with each new day, I move closer to living my life as *authentically mine.*

Recently, I read an article by Bronnie Ware called "Nurse reveals top 5 regrets people make on their deathbed." The study showed that a high percentage of people regret that they didn't laugh more, that they lived the lives that others wanted for them, and that they worked at jobs that did not inspire them enough. If today were my last day, I would not want to leave this world filled with regrets, sorrow, or bitterness for having lived based on what others thought was right or best for me. Most days, I wake up hungry for another day filled with self-discovery and embracing all that I truly desire.

The thought—what if this is my last day?—has been a strong motivator for me for a number of years. I stepped into this experience for the first time (that I recall) when I was fresh out of high school. My two-year relationship had just ended, I was heading off to university, and the world was mine to explore.

For the most part, the idea that the world was mine to explore scared the hell out of me. I decided that summer to create a bucket list to put in writing all the things I dreamed of experiencing and all the places I longed to visit. This list, this activity, this habit has served me well. It served as a reminder and helped focus and motivated me to get out and discover my world. My bucket list inspired me go whitewater rafting in Ottawa, Austria, and Costa Rica, travel to more than thirty countries (one summer with backpack in hand, I spent six weeks traveling Europe), parasailing (Greece and Florida), scuba diving (Florida and Cuba), fired a gun (a Glock, a Winchester, and a sniper), rode on a Harley (three times), took salsa and Lindy Hop dance lessons (for two years), rode in a small plane (over Go Home Lake Ontario and across the center of Costa Rica), hiked up Mount Chirripó (Costa Rica), stayed in an eco lodge in the rainforest (Costa Rica), did humanitarian work and a safari in Kenya, explored Ireland by myself, took surf lessons (Ireland and California), danced in the rain, sang karaoke, and went hang gliding. The list has had spontaneous items added to it over the years such skydiving tandem and solo (Ontario and Ireland), zip lining (Jamaica), and taking a helicopter ride (over Disney in Florida).

As I look back, I am aware that there are significant gaps in my life where I seem to have forgotten and my life has fallen into the routine and the busyness of the day-to-day life. I wonder how it was possible to forget about my bucket list since it has always brought me so much joy. How could I go two years without accomplishing or adding a single item to my list? Do I need an everyday live-life-fully list?

I keep reading that the little things make all the difference. It is about building daily habits that change one's landscape. I have started another bucket list. Thinking of the possibilities makes me smile. In addition to a bucket list of adventures, I am creating daily habits to remind me and help me focus on what I value in my life. I hope I won't get lost in the routines or expectations of others.

In the past months, I have been able to dig deep. I am getting a clearer picture as to what I value, desire, and want in my life. When my last day comes, I want to look back on my life and feel joy in the memories. I want to be satisfied, delighted, and proud of who I am and what I have done in this precious short life of mine.

My hope for you:
Dream and dream big.
Then give it all you got to make those dreams your life.
Enjoy the journey.
And may your life be filled with much
Freedom,
Vulnerability, and
Love!

To continue this journey together or to explore how I may further support and serve you, please visit www.kathybazinet.com

About the Author

Kathy Bazinet has worked in the self-help, consulting and coaching field for many years and has been on an active journey of self discovery for most of her life. She lives with her two daughters, both of whom have taught her much about love, laughter and play. In addition to her newly found love of writing, Kathy enjoys hiking, indoor climbing, travel and new adventures.

CPSIA information can be obtained at www.ICGtesting.com
Printed in the USA
BVOW07s0355230714

360110BV00001B/6/P